THE FABULOUS LOST & FOUND

AND THE LITTLE MALTESE MOUSE

WRITTEN BY MARK PALLIS
ILLUSTRATED BY PETER BAYNTON

**NEU WESTEND
— PRESS —**

For John and MaryRose - MP

For Hannah and Skye - PB

THE FABULOUS LOST & FOUND AND THE LITTLE MALTESE MOUSE
Copyright text © 2020 Mark Pallis and Copyright images © 2020 Peter Baynton

Maltese translation: Ruben Farrugia

All rights reserved. This book or any portion thereof may not be reproduced or used in any manner whatsoever without the express written permission of the publisher except for the use of brief excerpts in a review.

First Printing 2020
ISBN: 978-1-913595-13-5
NeuWestendPress.com

THE FABULOUS LOST & FOUND

AND THE LITTLE MALTESE MOUSE

WRITTEN BY MARK PALLIS
ILLUSTRATED BY PETER BAYNTON

NEU WESTEND
— PRESS —

In the middle of the big city is a tiny yellow building. If anyone loses anything, this is where it ends up.

It is called the Lost and Found.

Mr and Mrs Frog keep everything safe, hoping that someday every lost watch and bag and phone and toy and shoe and cheesegrater will find its owner again.

But the shop is very small. And there are so many lost things. It is all quite a squeeze, but still, it's fabulous.

One sunny day, a little mouse walked in.

"Welcome," said Mrs Frog. "What have you lost?"

"Tlift il-kappell tiegħi," said the mouse.

Mr and Mrs Frog could not speak Maltese. They had no idea what the little mouse was saying.

What shall we do? they wondered.

Maybe she's lost an umbrella. Everyone loses an umbrella at least twice, thought Mr Frog.

"Have you lost this?" asked Mr Frog.

"Dik umbrella? Le," replied the mouse.

Then Mrs Frog remembered something that had been handed in a few months ago...

"Is this yours?" Mrs Frog asked, holding up a chunk of cheese.

"Gobon? Le. Kemm jinten!" said the mouse.

"Time to put that cheese in the bin dear," said Mr Frog.

"Maybe the word 'kappell' means coat," said Mr Frog.

"Now where did I put that nice yellow one?"

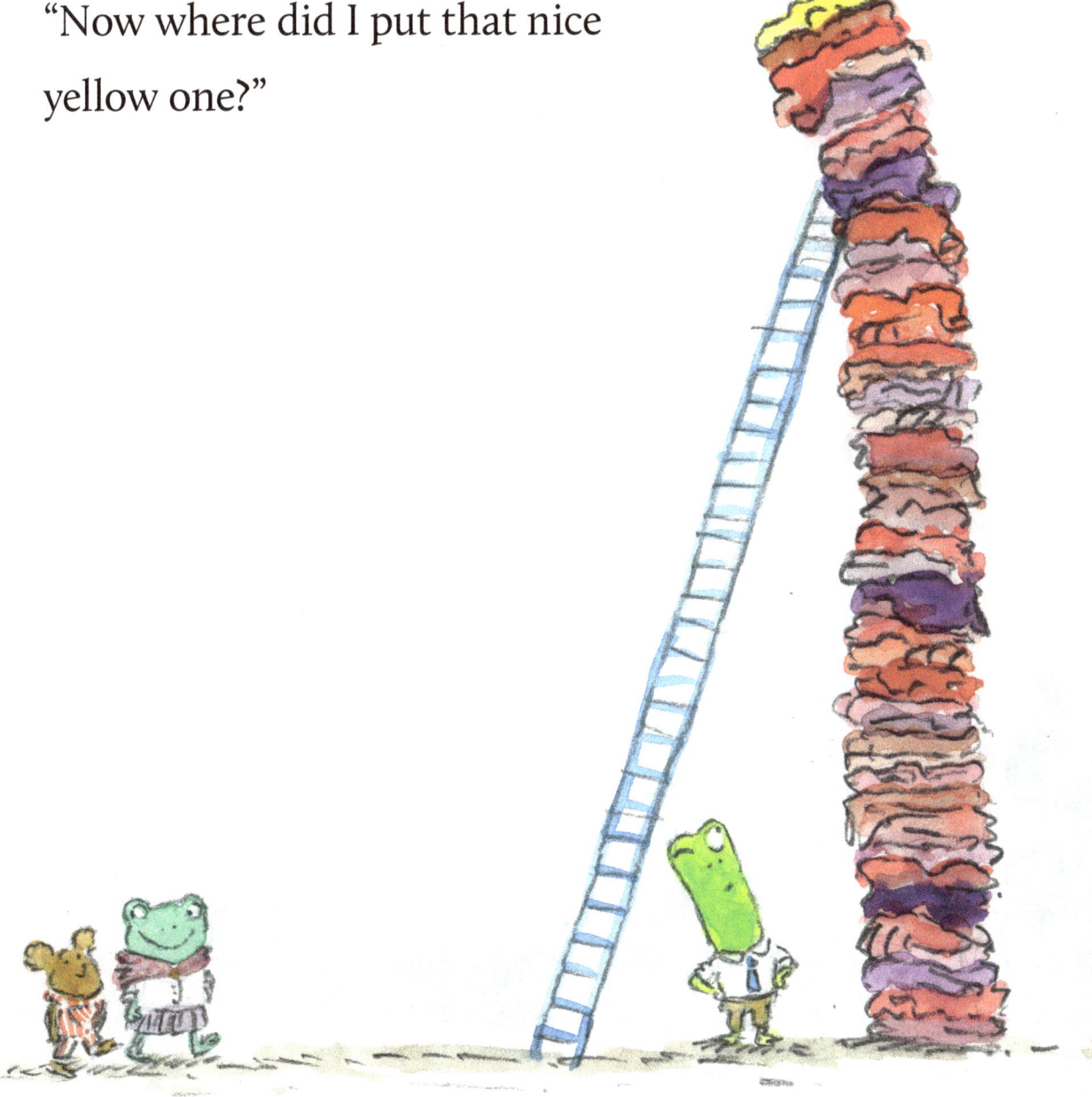

"Got it!" said Mr Frog.

"Kowt? Le. Tlift il-kappell tiegħi,"
                    said the mouse.

She was starting to feel a bit frustrated.

"We need to keep trying," said Mrs Frog.

Mhix xalpa.

Mhux qalziet.

Mhux ġerżi.

Mhux nuċċali tax-xemx.

Mhux żarbun.

"Tlift il-kappell tiegħi," said the mouse.

Mhumiex żewġ roti.

Mhux kompjuter.

Mhumiex tliet kotba.

Mhux erba' bananiet.

Mhumiex ħames ċwievet.

It was no good. A fat wet tear rolled down the mouse's cheek.

"How about a nice cup of tea?" asked Mrs Frog kindly.

"Joghgobni t-te. Grazzi," replied the mouse. They sat together, sipping their tea and all feeling a bit sad.

Suddenly, the mouse realised she could try pointing.

She pointed at her head. "Kappell!" she said.

"I've got it!" exclaimed Mrs Frog, leaping up.

"A wig of course!" said Mrs Frog.

"Mhix parrokka," said the mouse.

Mhix ħamra.

Mhix bjonda.

Mhix kannella.

Mhix mimlija kuluri.

Mhix ħadra.

"What about this?" asked Mr Frog, pulling back a curtain.

"Kappell!" exclaimed the mouse.

"Ah, so 'kappell' means hat. Wonderful!" Mr and Mrs Frog cheered.

Twil wisq.

Żgħir wisq.

Kbir wisq.

Issikkat wisq.

"One hat left," said Mrs Frog, reaching all the way to the back of the cupboard.

"It couldn't be this old thing, could it?"

"Il-kappell tiegħi.

Sibt il-kappell tiegħi!

Grazzi ħafna," said the mouse.

And just like that, the mouse found her hat.

"Saħħa" she said, as she skipped away.
"Saħħa," replied Mr and Mrs Frog.

"I wonder who will come tomorrow?" said Mr Frog.
Mrs Frog put her arm around him.

"I don't know," she replied, giving him a squeeze,
"but whoever it is, we'll do our best to help."

LEARNING TO LOVE LANGUAGES

An additional language opens a child's mind, broadens their horizons and enriches their emotional life. Research has shown that the time between a child's birth and their sixth or seventh birthday is a "golden period" when they are most receptive to new languages. This is because they have an in-built ability to distinguish the sounds they hear and make sense of them. The Story-powered Language Learning Method taps into these natural abilities, makes learning fun and builds confidence.

HOW THE STORY-POWERED LANGUAGE LEARNING METHOD WORKS

We create an emotionally engaging and funny story for children and adults to enjoy together, just like any other picture book. Studies show that social interaction, like enjoying a book together, is critical in language learning.

Through the story, we introduce a relatable character who speaks only in the new language. This helps build empathy and a positive attitude towards people who speak different languages. These are both important aspects in laying the foundations for lasting language acquisition in a child's life.

As the story progresses, the child naturally works with the characters to discover the meaning of a wide range of fun new words. Strategic use of humour ensures that this subconscious learning is rewarded with laughter; the child feels good and the first seeds of a lifelong love of languages are sown.

For more information and free downloads visit www.neuwestendpress.com

ALL THE BEAUTIFUL MALTESE WORDS AND PHRASES FROM OUR STORY

Maltese	English
Tlift il-kappell tiegħi	I've lost my hat
umbrella	umbrella
ġobon	cheese
jinten!	stinks!
kowt	coat
xalpa	scarf
qalziet	trousers
nuċċali tax-xemx	sunglasses
ġerżi	jumper
żarbun	shoe
wieħed	one
tnejn	two
tlieta	three
erbgħa	four
ħamsa	five
kompjuter	computer
ktieb	book
ċavetta	key
rota	bicycle
jogħġobni t-te	I like tea
grazzi	thank you
parrokka	wig
ħamra	red
bjonda	blond
kannella	brown
ħadra	green
mimlija kuluri	multicoloured
le	no
kappell	hat
twil wisq	too tall
kbir wisq	too big
żgħir wisq	too small
issikkat wisq	too tight
sibt il-kappell tiegħi	I've found my hat
grazzi ħafna	thank you very much
saħħa	goodbye

THE WORLD OF
THE FABULOUS LOST & FOUND

THIS STORY IS ALSO AVAILABLE IN...

TAGALOG
SPANISH
ITALIAN
CZECH
KOREAN
WELSH
GERMAN
HEBREW
SWEDISH
POLISH
SLOVAKIAN
VIETNAMESE
LATIN
PORTUGUESE

...AND MANY MORE LANGUAGES!

ENJOYED IT?
WRITE A REVIEW AND
LET US KNOW!

@MARK_PALLIS ON TWITTER
WWW.MARKPALLIS.COM

@PETERBAYNTON ON INSTAGRAM
WWW.PETERBAYNTON.COM

www.ingramcontent.com/pod-product-compliance
Lightning Source LLC
Chambersburg PA
CBHW051250110526
44588CB00025B/2939